Canine
Shenanigans

Books by Nancy L. Reed

Conversations Between Two Great Friends

A Short Story Olio

Questions: so many questions

Dog-grr-el: canine cadence, hound haiku, puppy poetry

Dog-grr-el: canine conundrums, hound hankerings, puppy puzzlers

Words Left Behind: tales from a life gladly lived

Satellite Cooking: main meals with spin-off recipes

Upcoming Books by Nancy L. Reed

The Ages and Stages of One Woman's Poetry:
from childhood imagination to teen angst to adult contemplation to senior serendipity

More Words Left Behind: still afloat

Animal Antics: from Albatrosses to Zebras

Canine
Shenanigans
from Afghans to Zuchons

Nancy L. Reed

Copyright© 2021 by Nancy L. Reed

All rights reserved.
This book or any portion thereof may not be reproduced or used in any manner whatsoever without the express written permission of the author or publisher.

Printed in the United States of America.
First Edition, 2021
Wabi Sabi Publishing LLC

Cover Design
Jennifer Schafer

Illustrations
Jennifer Schafer

ISBN: 978-0-9600999-8-6

Dedication

To all lovers of words and those who like to play with them.

Disclaimer

This is a work of fiction. Names, characters, businesses, places, events and incidents are either the products of the author's imagination or used in a fictitious manner. Any resemblance to actual persons, living or dead, or actual places or events is purely coincidental. Any resemblance to existent verse is unintentional.

Only admiration and love were intended for all dog breeds mentioned.

Acknowledgments

A very large thanks to Jennifer Schafer for once again making my illustration wishes come true.

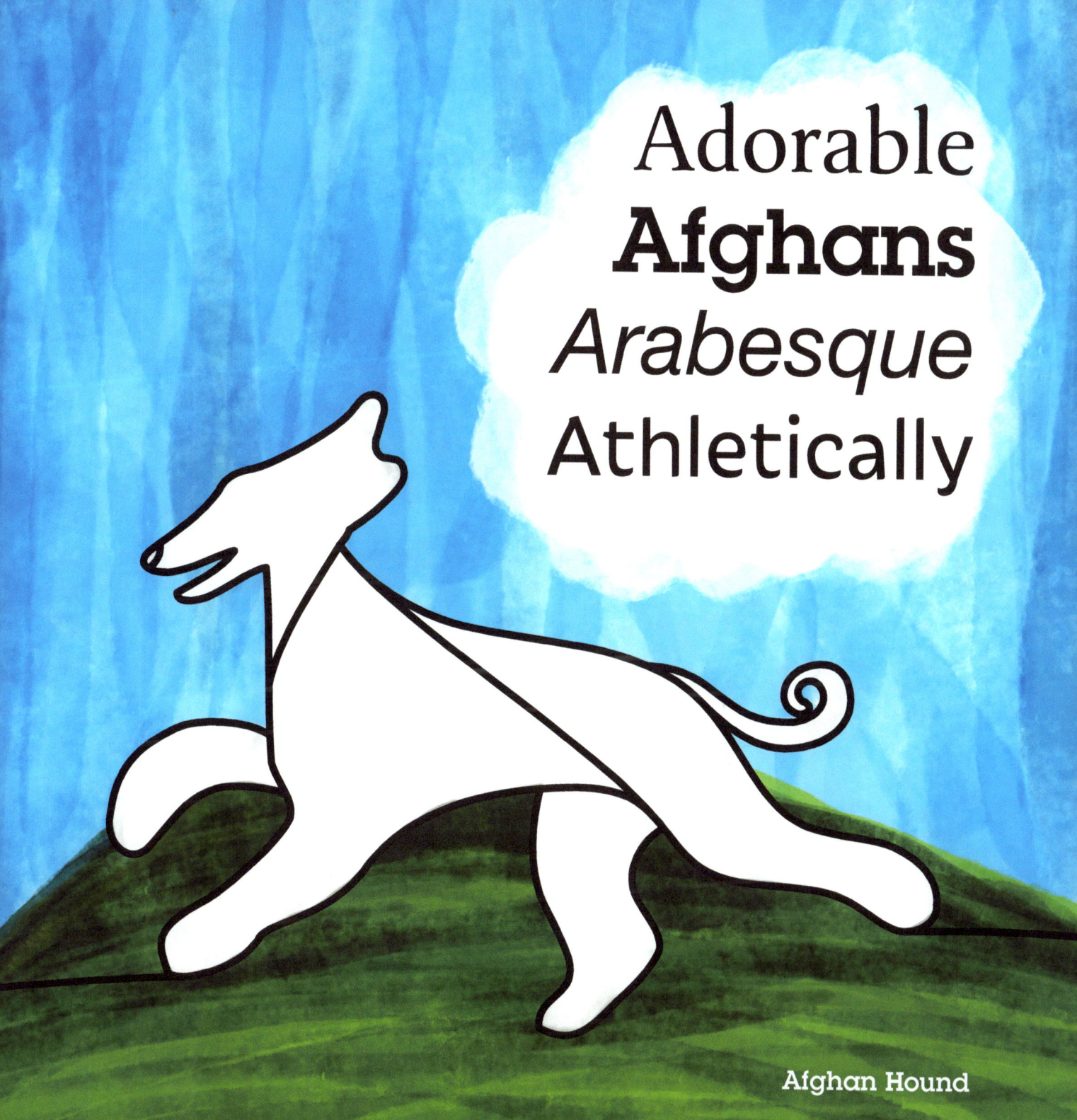

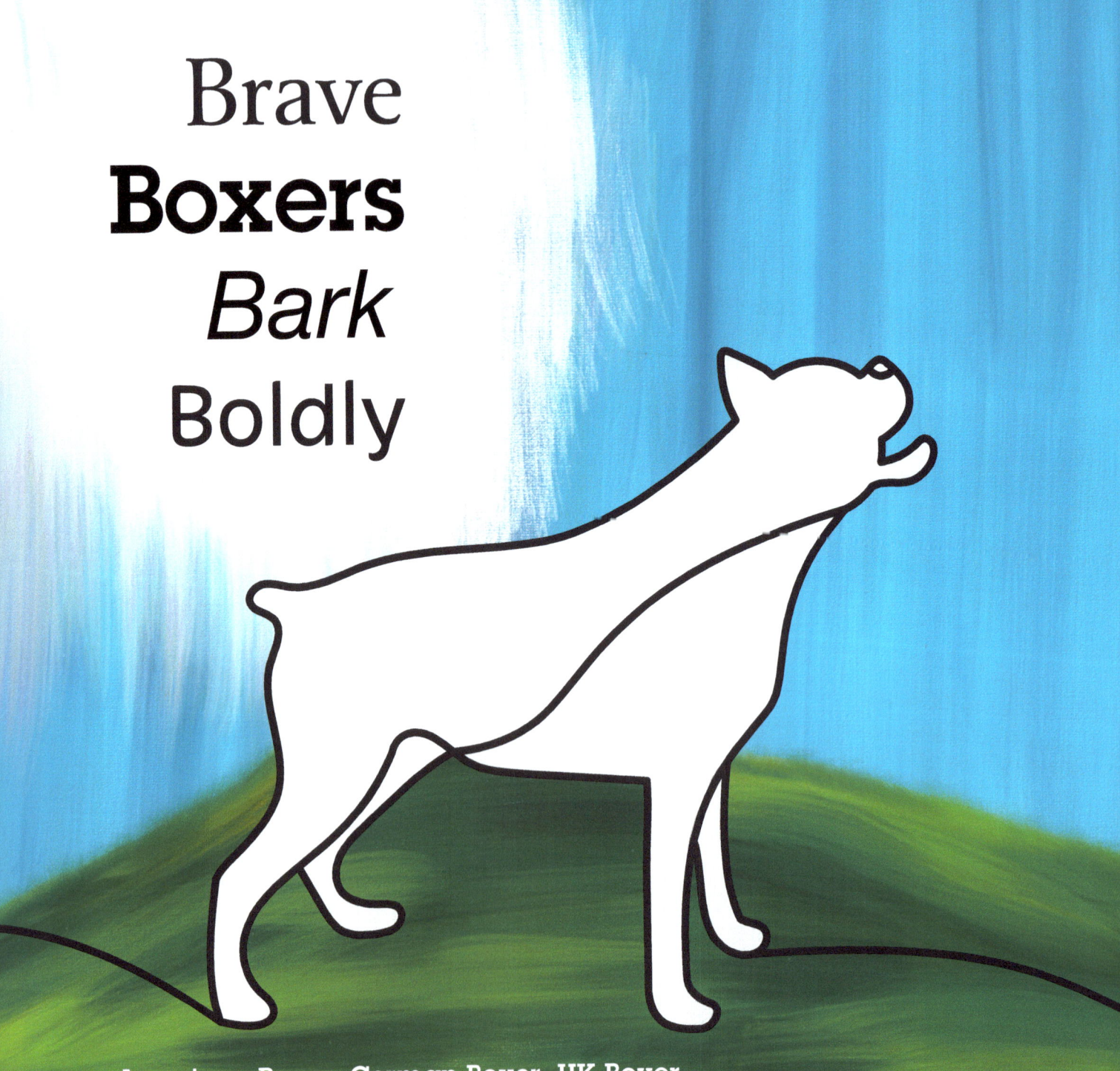

Cute **Corgis** *Congregate* Closely

Cardigan Welsh Corgi, Pembroke Welsh Corgi

Dizzy **Dalmatians** *Dance* Delightfully

English Coach Dog, Carriage Dog, Plum Pudding Dog

Elegant **Elkhounds** *Exercise* Energetically

Norwegian Elkhound

Graceful **Greyhounds** *Gallop* Gladly

Italian Greyhound

Jolly **Jafoxes** *Jostle* Jovially

Cross of 2 breeds: e.g. Japanese Chin with Fox Terrier, and other crosses

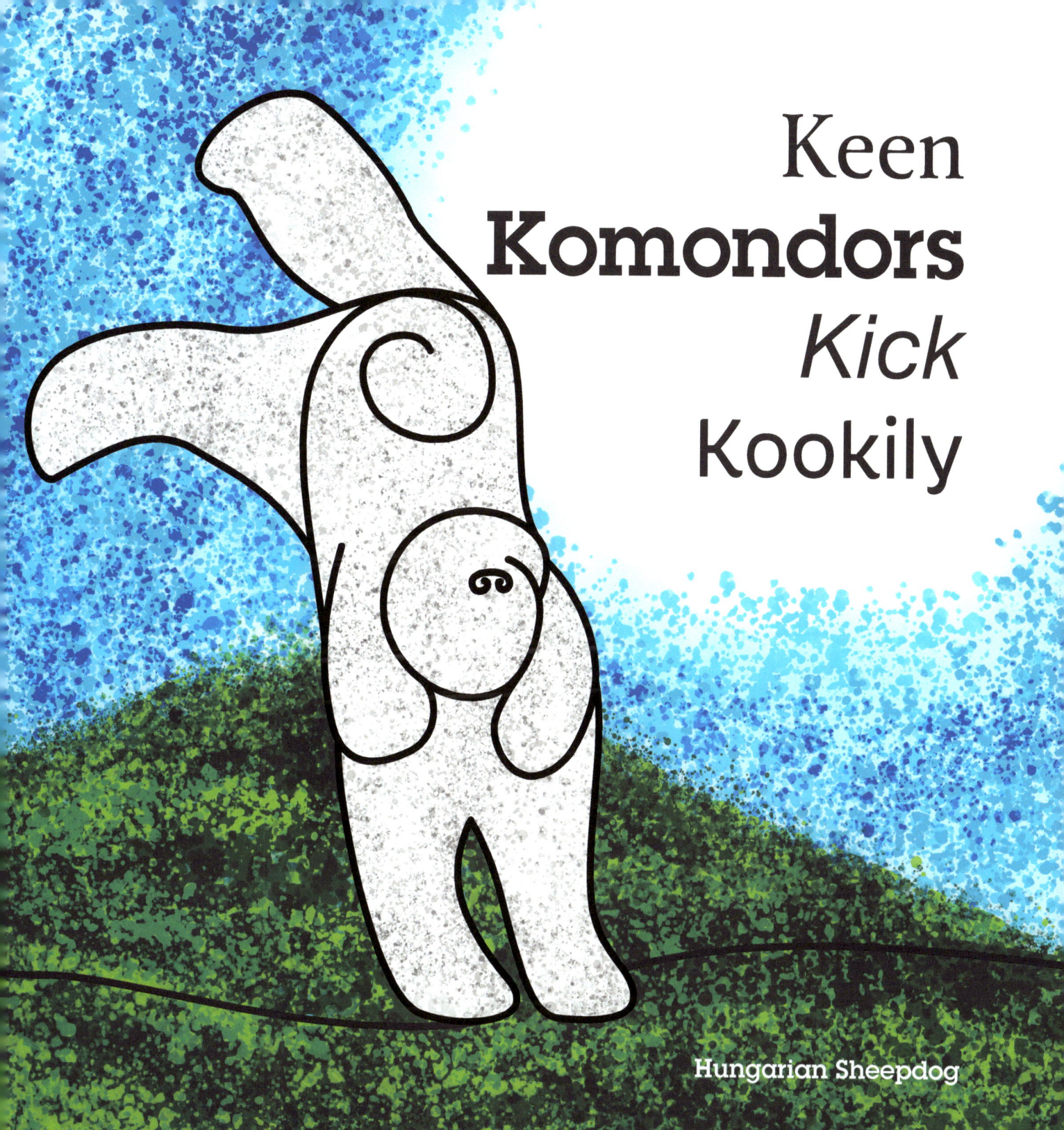

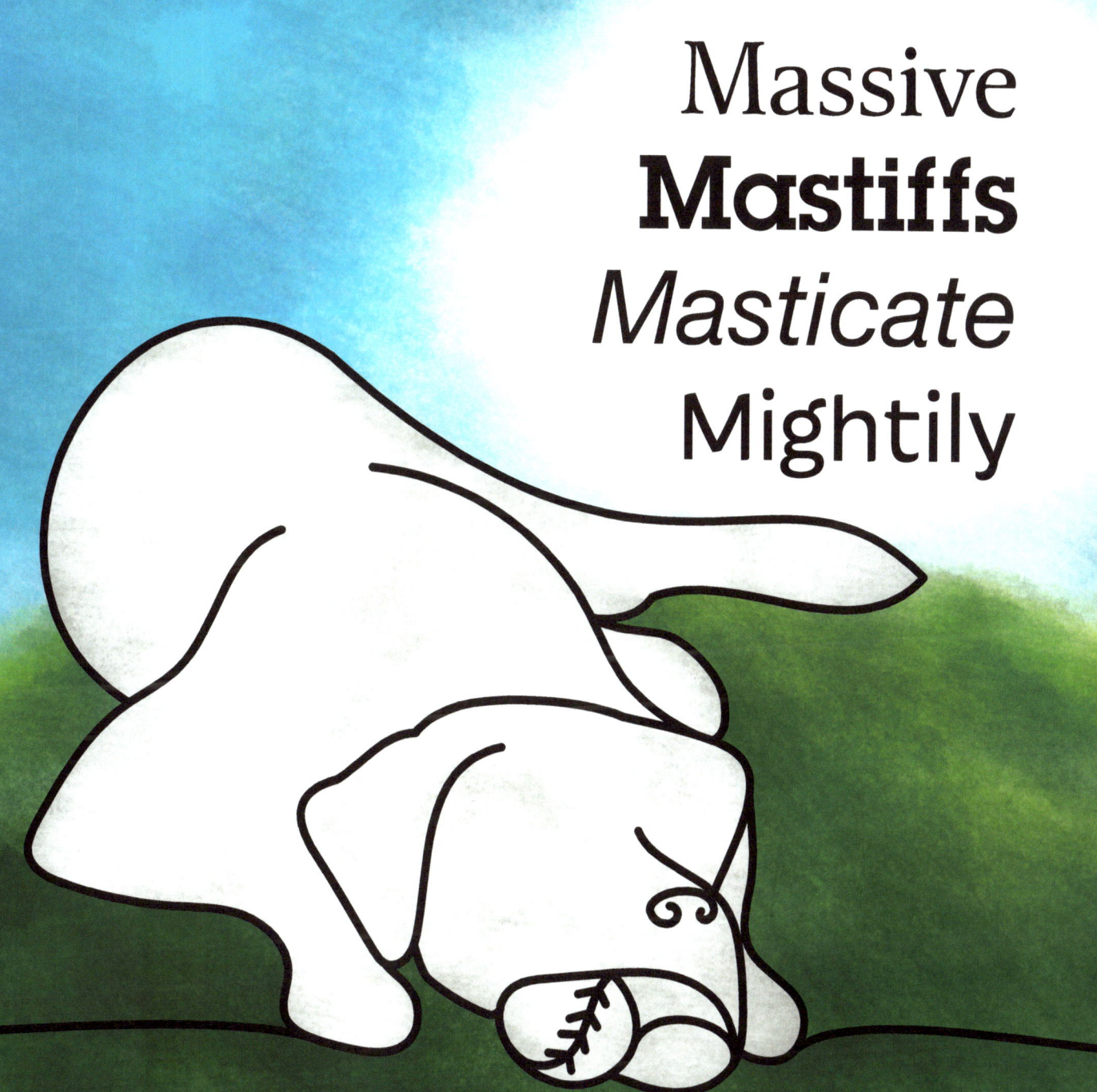

Massive **Mastiffs** *Masticate* Mightily

American Mastiff, English Mastiff, Bullmastiff, Tibetan Mastiff, and more

Natty
Newfoundlands
Nuzzle
Nicely

Lovingly called Newfies

Offbeat **Otterhounds** *Oscillate* Openheartedly

Cross of Bloodhound and several rough-coated French hound breeds

Quirky Queenslands Quickstep Quietly

Queensland Heeler, Australian Cattle Dog, Blue Heeler, and more

Rambunctious **Rottweilers** *Roll* Raucously

American Rottweiler, Roman Rottweiler, and more

Sweet Samoyeds Snuggle Sleepily

Lovingly called Sammies

Tenacious **Terriers** *Tease* Tauntingly

Airedale Terrier, American Staffordshire Terrier, and more

Shining **Xolos*** *Share* Showily

* Xoloitzcuintle (pronounced: sho-low-eets-KWEENT-lee)

Xoloitzcuintle, Mexican Hairless, Hairless Xolo, Coated Xolo

Young Yorkies Yap Youthfully

Yorkshire Terrier

Zippy Zuchons Zigzag Zestfully

Cross of 2 breeds: Bichon Frise and Shih Tzu

www.ingramcontent.com/pod-product-compliance
Lightning Source LLC
Chambersburg PA
CBHW040020050426
42452CB00002B/65